T0045230

Look How Tall I Am!

Tessa Patel
Illustrated by Teresa Culkin-Lawrence

We have a growth chart
at our house. We use it
to measure how tall we are.

5
4
men6
5
en3
3
Carmen2
Ben 2
2
Ben 1
Carmen1
Ryan 1
1

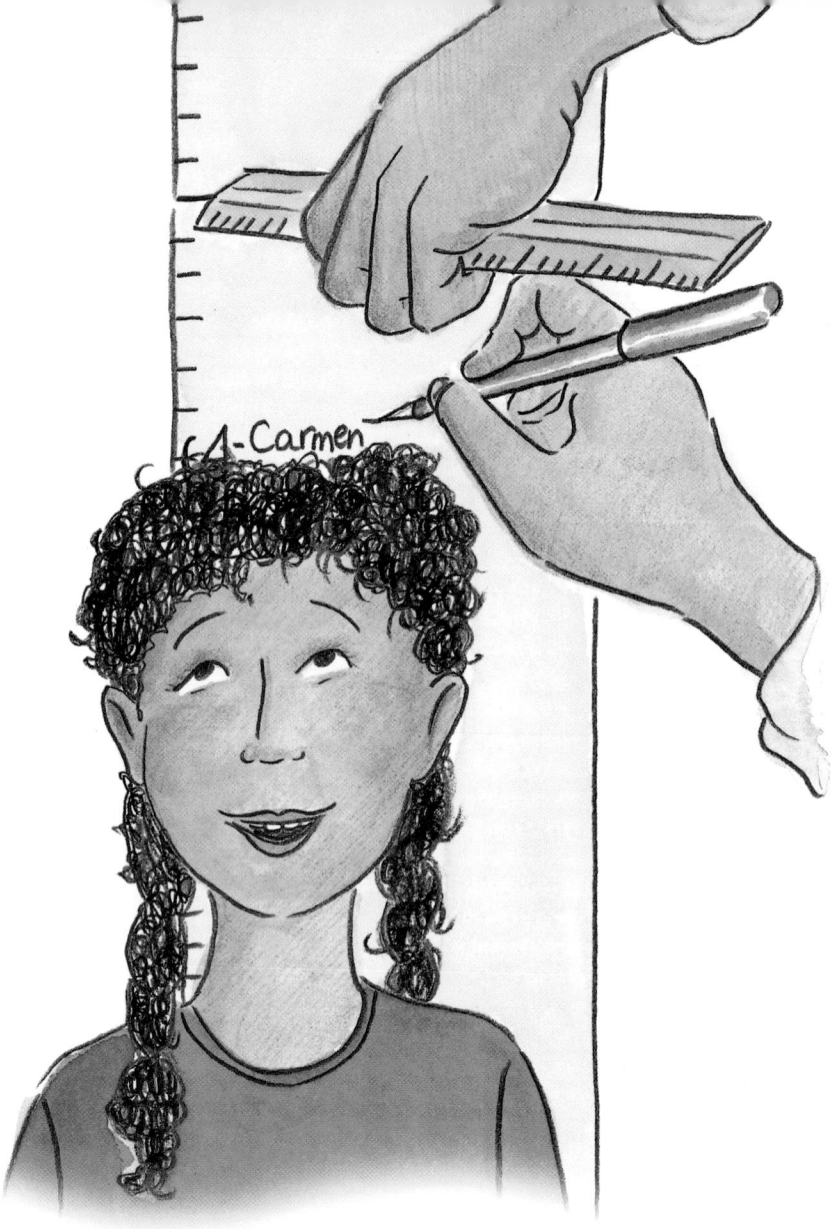

Dad measures me.

"Look how tall I am!" I say.

"Now it's Ben's turn," says Dad.

Dad measures Ben.

"Look how tall I am!" says Ben.

"Now it's Ryan's turn," I say.
Dad measures Ryan.

"Look how tall I am!" says Ryan.

"Carmen is the tallest," says Ben. "Ryan and I are both shorter than Carmen!"

4 Carmen 7
Carmen 6
Ben 5
Carmen 5
Carmen 4
Ben 3
3
Ryan 3
Carmen 2
Ben 2
2
Ben 1
Carmen 1
Ryan 1
1

"We will see about that," laughs Dad.
He puts Ryan on Ben's shoulders.

I stand next to Ben and Ryan.
I laugh, "Now I'm the shortest!"

6
5

"But Dad is the tallest of all!"
we say.